Forever
SQUAM

Forever SQUAM

Photography by

ROBERT J. KOZLOW

HUNTINGTON GRAPHICS
Burlington, Vermont

Huntington Graphics
PO Box 373, Burlington, VT 05402
www.huntingtongraphics.com

ISBN 978-1-886064-52-2

Contents

The early morning sun rises on a calm Squam Lake reflecting Red Hill in the distance.

Acknowledgments

Many people were instrumental in the creation of this book. Jared Gange, my publisher, reviewed the manuscript and images and his designer, Andrea Gray, spent many hours placing the images to provide a striking artistic representation of Squam Lake. My friend, Chris Whiton reviewed all images and adjusted them for proper printing resolution.

I would especially like to thank Roger Larochelle of Squam Lakes Conservation Society for writing the "Forever Squam" introduction and his assistance with the chapter headings.

I would like to take the time to recognize the many property owners and care-takers on Squam who gave me permission to obtain images from unique viewpoints. In particular, I would like to thank Scott Nason, Davis Keniston, David Burns, and the Young, Keefer, Van Winkle, Murphy, Coolidge, Conover, and Lawler families. I would also like to acknowledge Andrew and Patrick Keefer, Cindy O'Leary, Tod Campbell and John Barry for providing me with boat rides to get to some beautiful destinations on the lake.

Special thanks go to all my friends who helped me with various photo shoots and who appear as models throughout this book. Most notably, I would like to thank Andrew and Patrick Keefer who introduced me to the beauty of this lake and have been on a number of modeling assignments for me. In addition, I would like to thank Spencer Pickering, Martin Kimball, Eric Morse, Tod Campbell, Wesley Gunselman, David Badura and Billy Noble

I would like to thank David Emerson, Staci Schoenrock and Bryan Rivillas of Emerson Aviation for assistance in obtaining the aerial photos as well as Patrick Keefer and Tod Campbell for assistance in obtaining loon photos.

I am very fortunate to have professional colleagues who have supported me through all my photography projects. In particular, I'd like to thank Dr. Olga Minukhin and the Dental Resource Center team at LRGHealthcare as well as my Meredith dental office team. Thank you, Kelly Beddia, for being such a good listener and faithful friend over all these years.

Finally, I would like to dedicate this book to my parents, the late Donna and Joseph Kozlow, whose unconditional love, patience and encouragement made all of this possible. It has truly been a labor of love on many wonderful journeys through God's country.

Robert J. Kozlow
Gilford, New Hampshire

A quintessential Squam Lake cottage on a calm summer morning at sunrise.

Preface

When I first moved to New Hampshire over twenty years ago, I remember taking my parents on a wonderful tour boat operated by the Squam Lakes Natural Science Center. It was my first boat trip on Squam and it was entertaining to hear the history of the lake and sights associated with the movie, "On Golden Pond." Never would I have known that I would fall in love with this "jewel" of the Lakes Region some twenty years later.

Squam Lake is my favorite New Hampshire lake. It's that simple! The reason I believe Squam is so special is that it is unique in two significant ways. Not only does it have spectacular beauty but more importantly, it is well preserved and undeveloped. Squam Lakes Region is a two-hour drive from Boston yet the area has not experienced the extensive commercial or residential development that has ravaged so many other lakes in this region. The Squam Lakes Association and the Squam Lakes Conservation Society have played an important role in conserving and protecting this unique region so that you will not find any condominium developments, motels, marinas or other commercial establishments on Big Squam Lake. The reluctance to alter the landscape is an early tradition established by the owners of older Squam camps and is reinforced by the Rockywold and Deephaven camps which have remained unchanged for a century. There is an unspoken ethic for anyone associated with Squam to preserve and protect the lake.

I will never forget my first boat trip to Yard Island with my friend, Andrew Keefer. Imagine a sandy beach with turquoise colored water reminiscent of a Caribbean island in the middle of a New Hampshire lake. I was mesmerized by this island and it has been one of my favorite spots on Squam ever since. I firmly believe that Squam needs to be explored in all four seasons to truly appreciate its scenic splendor and wild nature.

This poem by Henry David Thoreau best describes my feelings for Squam.

> I long for wilderness
> Woods where the wood thrush
> Forever sings
> Where the hours are early
> Morning ones
> And the dew is on the grass
> And the day is forever
> Unproven
> A New Hampshire everlasting
> And unfallen

Robert J. Kozlow
May 2018

Sunset in Squaw Cove.

Forever Squam

Forever Squam...this is the mission of the Squam Lakes Conservation Society.

As Squam's Land Trust, we've been working toward forever for a long, long time. Protecting Squam's special places is more than just conserving land; it is about ensuring that the character of this special community endures.

Dr. Kozlow has a special gift for capturing the timeless spirit of this place and community. His images transcend time and reach across everyday experiences to inspire us and connect us to the awe and majesty of Squam's land, lake, and people.

Squam is, without doubt, a beautiful and unique place. We are grateful that part of the proceeds of this book will help permanently protect more of Squam. Investing in its protection will allow the place we treasure today to remain intact and recognizable for all the generations to come.

Here's to helping it remain that way forever.

Roger Larochelle
Executive Director
Squam Lakes Conservation Society

Bird's Eye View

Soaring high above the lakes and mountains, Squam's Bald Eagles have a special vantage point as the foothills of the White Mountains yield to the most northern of New Hampshire's large lakes. Squam Lake is the second largest lake in New Hampshire, but it is first in the hearts of many. An aerial perspective gives us a unique view of Squam and its thirty-one islands and scenic coves.

A summer aerial view of Squam Lake with the Sandwich Range and White Mountains in the background.

"Ice-out" can occur any time from late March to early May. Sandwich Bay is usually the last area to ice out. Hubble Island (lower left), Three Sisters Islands (lower right), and Long Island (center) are seen in this image.

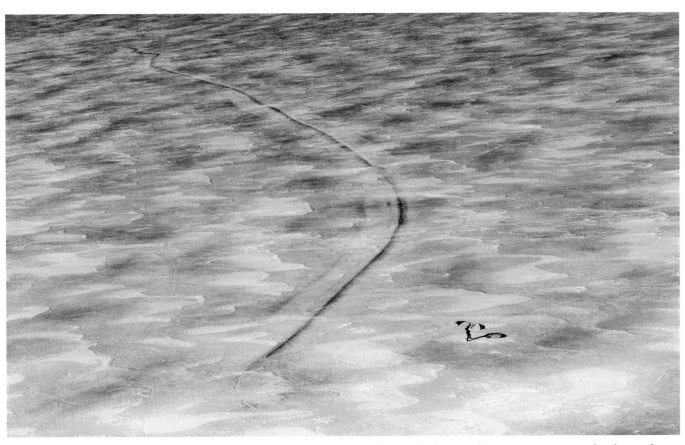

An aerial view of a kitewinger on Squam Lake. Many parts of the lake can have ice thicknesses of seventeen to twenty inches during the winter months.

Summer aerial view of Squam Lake looking southeast from high above Willoughby Ridge.

Summer aerial view of Big Squam, Little Squam, and White Oak Pond.

This unique spring aerial view of Yard Islands show the shallow rocky nature of the lake around the islands.

Winter view of Squam Lake with Mount Washington and the White Mountains in the distance.

Aerial view of Squam Lake during peak fall foliage with snowcapped Mount Washington in the distance.

An aerial view of Squam's most scenic coves. Squaw Cove (lower left), Bear Cove (Center), and Rattlesnake Cove (lower right) are some of the most beautiful and peaceful areas on the lake due to their no wake zones.

On the Water

Whether it is taking a paddle, cruising on the Squam Lakes Natural Science Center pontoon boat, swimming in the lake's cool clear waters, or skimming across the ice with a kitewing, there is something on Squam Lake for everyone. The best time to be on the lake is at sunrise or sunset, where one can experience quiet peace and awesome beauty often accompanied by the haunting sounds of the loons.

The cottage scene from the movie, "On Golden Pond," was filmed from this land extension and boathouse off of Center Harbor Neck. A portion of Great Island is visible on the left side of this image.

Loons, like most water birds, need to shake water from their feathers from time to time.

Squam Lake is a nesting site for common loons. In early July, loon chicks will ride on their mother's back for a short while until they become strong enough to swim on their own.

This swimmer is about to create a big splash on an otherwise calm Rattlesnake Cove.

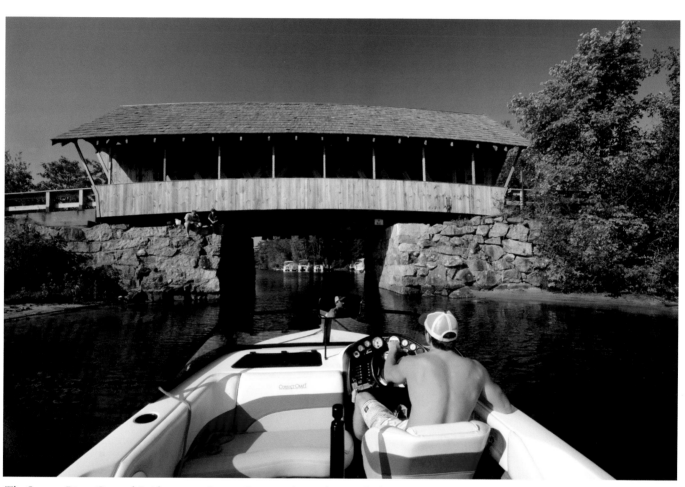

The Squam River Covered Bridge crosses Squam River at the southern end of Little Squam Lake in Ashland.

Sunrise from Willoughby Point. Some of the most magnificent sunrises can be seen on Squam from various locations on the western end of the lake.

The two islets of Squaw Cove are highlighted by the sun on a particularly calm and cloudy afternoon.

Moonrise over Red Hill on the night of a full moon at Yard Island.

A new day dawns at Yard Island.

A perfect reflection of Squaw Cove with East Rattlesnake Mountain in the distance.

Yard Island winter sunset.

Sailboat Regatta on Squam. Each Sunday in July and August, Squam sailboat enthusiasts gather for these afternoon races.

Aerial view of sailboats on Squam.

A lone bob-house in Sandwich Bay at sunset.

With the setting sun over Sandwich Bay, the lake takes on a honeycomb appearance as pieces of ice break up in preparation for "ice-out."

On the Land

Squam Lake is surrounded by the towns of Holderness, Sandwich, Moultonborough, Center Harbor, and Ashland. Each town has its own unique character and all share a rural farming history. Each season brings a refreshing beauty to the land, whether it be a heavy wet snow covering the tree branches after a winter storm, or the yellow-green buds and flowers that give life to the landscape in the spring. Summer shows off the dark greens of the trees with wild day lilies adorning fields and homesteads and autumn brings forth a burst of red and orange to the trees.

Lilac is the official state flower of New Hampshire and usually blooms during late May. These lilacs are adorning the historic homesteads in Center Sandwich.

A lone oak tree near Sandwich Notch gets its first rays of winter sunlight.

Early morning fog at Burleigh Farm in Holderness.

Spring is ushered in by the presence of lupine in Grapevine Cove.

A lone standing oak tree near Sandwich Notch comes alive with a field of dandelions.

True Farm Pond reflects the stillness of this pastoral setting.

In early May, the hills are alive with daffodils at Cotton Farm in Moultonborough.

Wild day lilies adorn this field in Center Sandwich overlooking the Sandwich Range.

The stillness of this scene hints at the timelessness of the well preserved village of Center Sandwich.

Oranges and reds are ablaze near the Burleigh Farm in Holderness.

An oak tree near Sandwich Notch shows off peak color while the upper elevations are sporting a change from fall to winter.

Apple blossoms burst forth in mid-May on this farm in Sandwich with Red Hill in the distance.

Spring has sprung at Burleigh Farm in Holderness.

Burleigh Farm decked out for the Christmas season.

A quintessential New England barn in Sandwich is adorned with candles and wreaths for the holiday season.

On the Trail

Over fifty miles of trails provide a wide range of experiences and habitat for hikers and explorers of all ages. The peaks of the Squam Range and West Rattlesnake are the most frequent destinations, but the area abounds in options. Beede Falls, off of Sandwich Notch Road, provides hikers with an opportunity to cool off under a waterfall after their long aerobic workout.

West Rattlesnake Mountain view overlooking Veerie Cove and Squam Lake.

Eagle Cliff Trail off of Red Hill offers a unique up-close perspective of Squam and the Five Finger Point Natural Area. The 0.6 mile trail off of Bean Road is steep and rocky but relatively easy to follow.

For a more expansive view of Squam Lake, one of the most beautiful viewpoints is from Mount Doublehead, which is part of the thirteen-mile Crawford-Ridgepole trail.

Chamberlain Reynolds Memorial Forest is a 157-acre land tract with over a mile of waterfront on Squam. There are several beaches, a swamp boardwalk, and over four miles of hiking trails. This sunset is from one of the several beaches on the property.

A popular short hike to West Rattlesnake Mountain on the night of a full moon leads to this spectacular vista over Squam Lake.

A breathtaking fall foliage view of Squam Lake from Mount Morgan. The lower peak on the far left is West Rattlesnake.

Contemplating the colorful fall foliage display surrounding Squam Lake from the summit of West Rattlesnake.

Spirit of Squam

The spirit and essence of Squam can be seen in many traditions, some of which date back over one hundred years, such as the Annual Ice Harvest at Rockywold-Deephaven and the Sandwich Fair, to some more recent traditions such as the Correct Craft Regatta Parade and the Sunday sailboat races. Each season has its own traditions such as maple sugaring, patriotic parades and fireworks, and celebrations during the holiday season.

From late February through the month of March, maple sugar operations are in full gear at Booty's Farm in Sandwich.

The ice harvest at Rockywold-Deephaven Camp is an annual tradition dating back over one hundred years.

The blocks of ice harvested from Squam Lake are brought to the icehouses at Rockywold-Deephaven and packed in sawdust until summer, when they are brought forth, still frozen, and placed in "ice-boxes" at the individual cottages during the summer months.

Correct Craft Regatta Parade at the channel connecting Big and Little Squam.

A vintage antique steamboat makes its way through the channel from Big Squam.

The Rockywold-Deephaven crew members line up to deliver ice blocks to each of the cottages at this well-known summer camp.

Each cottage at Rockywold-Deephaven is equipped with an "ice-box" that is kept cold with an ice block that was harvested in the winter. This tradition dates back over one hundred years.

The 250th Anniversary of the Town of Holderness, New Hampshire, was marked by the Mattatuck Fife and Drum Band, the oldest continuously existing band in the United States.

Fourth of July fireworks on Little Squam to celebrate our nation's independence.

What better way to celebrate the end of the harvest season than with french fries, fried dough, and a ferris wheel at the Sandwich Fair?

The first Sandwich Fair was held on Sunday, October 12th, 1909 and became a three-day event in 1988. It marks the end of the fall foliage season and the time when Squam owners visit their cottages and camps one final time before closing them down for the winter.

The Sandwich Creamery is a hidden gem tucked away in the woods of Sandwich. The creamery offers a variety of ice cream and cheeses and operates on the honor system of payment.

Chicks Corner School, a historic one-room school house in Sandwich, aglow on a cold winter night.

Christmas on a Squam Lake dock.

The Squam Boat Livery in Holderness is decked out for the holiday season.

Cottages, Camps, and Boathouses

Squam's rustic old camps and boathouses are a temple to the joy and purity of woodland living and a connector with our past. They are part of a unique American Heritage. The rustic camps and boathouses set Squam apart from many other lakes in the region because they are so well concealed behind trees that have been preserved along the shoreline, giving the lake a more wilderness feel.

The iconic Squam Boat Livery is in Holderness at the channel connecting Little Squam with Big Squam. The boathouse appeared in the movie "On Golden Pond."

A calm summer night is the perfect time for a campfire on Squam.

A typical summer camp on Squam with a hammock to enjoy the hazy, lazy days of summer.

"Red Lodge" – a "typical" cottage and boathouse on Squam Lake that has been enjoyed by several generations of family.

(OPPOSITE) *A quintessential summer lake cottage reflects the stillness of the early morning hours on Squam.*

Rockywold's rustic cottages nestled on Bennett Cove.

Deephaven Dock and the Studio are reflected in the calm waters off Needle Point.

There are several beautiful boathouses in the channel connecting Little and Big Squam.

This unique boathouse on Brown Point is adorned with flower boxes and a balcony.

The iconic Coolidge Boathouse in Sandwich Bay casts its reflection on the calm waters with Fore Point in the distance.

(OPPOSITE) *This iconic red boathouse is found at the end of the channel leading into Big Squam Lake.*

Islands and Coves

The shoreline of Squam Lake is as irregular as the lake bottom. Even experienced boaters *always* bring a chart for reefs and rocks that will inevitably greet them. Some of Squam's many inlets, coves, and islands maintain a no wake zone making them quieter and more peaceful. Each of the thirty one islands and numerous coves has its own unique character where one can find peace and tranquility.

The cross on the altar of Church Island is mirrored by the distant paddleboarder navigating the calm waters before sunrise.

Loon Island (left) and Little Loon Island (right) are seen in this spring reflection on a frozen Squam Lake.

Perch Island is one of the smaller, more picturesque islands located between Livermore Cove and Sunset Point.

A blast of fall color at Utopia Island.

Eastern end of Long Island at peak fall foliage.

Bowman Island (left) and Moon Island (right) are both owned by the Squam Lakes Association. Each island has campsites and docks which must be reserved months in advance due to their popularity.

Kent Island is located near Sandwich Bay.

Carnes Island on a foggy morning.

Hubble Island is located off Mooney Point and is next to Three Sisters Islands.

The Three Sisters are three islands located just south of Long Island. This particular island has a gazebo on the edge of its shore.

This is one of the Three Sisters Islands that has a picturesque rustic cabin on the edge of its shore.

The Yard Islands are a small group of tiny islands located near Harvard Point and High Haith. The lake is very shallow and rocky near the islands and beach area giving the water a Caribbean turquoise color.

Aerial view of Yard Islands.

Early morning calm on Nichols Cove.

Peak fall foliage on a calm morning in Bean Cove.

Adventures

Squam Lake presents limitless adventures year round. Winter brings opportunity for kitewinging, cross country skiing, ice skating, snowshoeing, ice sailing, ice fishing, and snowmobiling. Spring offers visits to local sugarhouses. Summer affords the lake lover boating, fishing, swimming, hiking, birdwatching, sailing, and paddle boarding. Fall brings out leaf peepers who come from all over the world to see our New England foliage.

A paddleboarder pauses to appreciate the beauty and promise of a sunrise on Squam.

Ice sailing is popular on Squam when the lake is covered with a solid layer of "black ice." Black ice is clear ice on a black surface.

Clear, glassy ice provides perfect conditions for pond hockey near Sandwich Bay.

Early morning fog in Squaw Cove provides a peaceful setting for a patient fisherman.

Although there are no "official" sled dog races on Squam, the lake provides a scenic backdrop for those interested in this sport.

A sailboat navigates the slightly windy conditions that are perfect for this sport.

A kayaker enjoys the quiet waters of Piper Cove, home of Squam Lakes Association.

A kitewinger takes flight near Loon Island on a beautiful winter day.

Kitewinging is an extremely popular sport on Squam. This kitewinger is riding the "river of wind" near Three Sisters Islands.

"Jumping Rock" is a popular spot in Rattlesnake Cove on a hot summer day.

The best time to waterski is early morning when the winds are calm and the lake takes on a glassy reflective surface.

A "Squambat" kitewinger rides the "river of wind" at sunset.

Cross-country skiers enjoy a traverse around frosted Yard Island.

Standing under Beede Falls is a great way to cool off after the quarter-mile hike in from Sandwich Notch Road.

For those who are adventurous, sliding down Beede Falls in an inner tube is a great way to cool off on a hot summer day.

Reflections

The tranquil beauty of Squam is best witnessed when there is complete calm and the lake mirrors the surrounding landscape. This often occurs before sunrise and after sunset. Many of the small coves and inlets remain calm due to no wake zones set up in those areas, making them ideal for reflections.

A perfectly calm spring day at the Webster Boathouse in Carnes Cove.

A perfect sunrise reflection from Willoughby Point. East Rattlesnake Mountain is on the left and Red Hill is on the right.

A moonrise image from Willoughby Point on the night before a full moon.

A dramatic winter sunrise from the channel entering Big Squam Lake.

A stellar moonrise over Red Hill from Cotton Cove.

The Old Mill site on Squam River in Ashland during peak fall foliage.

Sunrise brings endless possibilities for a perfect summer day on Squam.

Squaw Cove sunrise.

Squam begins the ice out process near small islands with numerous exposed rocks. The area near Yard Island is extremely shallow and it ices out before the deeper parts on the lake.

Sunrise near Jimmy Point overlooking Bear Cove.

The most vibrant and colorful sunrises occur just before a storm system is about to enter the region.

Kusumpe Pond in Sandwich is one of the few ponds in New Hampshire's Lakes Region with an entirely undeveloped shoreline. The area provides important habitat for loons, moose, bear, and song birds while providing visitors with opportunities to explore.

Intervale Pond in Sandwich is a hidden gem offering fishermen a variety of catches including brown trout, bullhead, smallmouth bass, largemouth bass, bream, and bluegill.

Sunrise in Rattlesnake Cove. May the peace and tranquility of Squam Lake fill your heart and soul!